W9-AQX-301

Picasso Linocuts 1958-1963

Exhibition Arranged by Trois Anges, Ltd., New York

Participating Museums:

Nelson Gallery—Atkins Museum, Kansas City

Herron Museum of Art, Indianapolis

Baltimore Museum of Art, Baltimore

Des Moines Art Center, Des Moines

Joslyn Art Museum, Omaha

Oklahoma Art Center, Oklahoma City

Washington University Gallery of Art, St. Louis

Museum of Fine Arts, Boston

PICASSO LINOCUTS 1958-1963

By Donald H. Karshan

THE COMPUTER APPLICATIONS INCORPORATED COLLECTION

Tudor Publishing Company, New York

The publisher gratefully acknowledges the courtesy of Computer Applications Incorporated, New York, for its cooperation in the production of this book.

Library of Congress Catalog Card Number: 68-56152

Printed in the United States of America

CONTENTS

PICASSO LINOCUTS 1958-1963

"To me a picture has always been a sum total of destructions"
—Pablo Picasso

Origin of the Linocut. First manufactured in 1860, linoleum is a universally used floor covering made by coating burlap with linseed oil, powdered cork and rosin. It is usually about one-quarter inch thick, and comes in large rolls, like carpeting. Pigments are added to create the desired colors and patterns—so maligned in our time as "linoleum designs." Because of its relative softness when cutting or gouging and its extremely low cost, however, there emerged in the 1920's a second use for this humble material—as a medium for making prints.

Like the woodblock, linoleum can serve as a simple "relief" printmaking device. The area that is not cut away, the original surface of the linoleum, picks up the rolled-on ink, which transfers onto paper when the block is hand-burnished or placed in a press. Small rectangles of linoleum glued to flat wooden blocks, usually not exceeding twelve by eight inches, are generally available from artists' and school supply stores. Nevertheless, the "linoleum cut" or "linocut" technique, as it is now described, continues to be used mainly in arts and crafts classes and by children. Who cannot remember with nostalgia as a child making a linoleum cut for a greeting card?

The linocut was considered too limited, too unsophisticated a method to be used by mature artists. There were a few exceptions to this general avoidance by the art community, one being Henri Matisse, whose *Head of a Woman* of 1938 (fig. 1) was then, in its utmost economy of white or "negative" line against black background, a recognition of the childlike simplicity of the medium. Another was Joan Miró, with a linocut of the same year. But those artists who created linocuts made few and they were nearly always of one color.

Figure 1.
Matisse: *Head of a Woman.*
Linocut. 1938.

This, then, was the general state of the linocut as a graphic art or multiple-image device through the early fifties, until a fortuitous combination of circumstances, and the ravenous aesthetic appetite of Pablo Picasso, turned this innocent technique into an innovation of the first magnitude, an invention of color-printing and printmaking vivacity that may well become the single most important contribution to twentieth-century graphic art.

Black and White for Half a Century. Picasso began his first long series of linocuts only in 1958, when he was seventy-seven years old. Aside from his prodigious output of paintings and sculpture by that time, he had also produced over two thousand prints since his first etching in 1897. By 1958, he was being described, and deservedly so, as the most accomplished graphic artist of our time. His masterpieces, *The Frugal Repast* of 1904, *The Minotauromachy* of 1935, the "Saltimbanque" series, published in 1913, the "Vollard Suite," completed in 1937, and the illustrations for Buffon's *Histoire naturelle,* published in 1942, among others, were all in the "intaglio" technique, whether etching, drypoint or aquatint. In all these processes, the indentations that are acid-etched, cut or scratched away from the copper plate receive the ink, while the original surface is wiped clean. The image is printed by pressing the paper into these recesses.

Although the most widely used relief process is the woodcut, Picasso had made only a few, an example being the *Young Woman Facing Left, Three-Quarter View* of 1906 (fig. 2). Apparently its slowness of execution and the difficulties of achieving tonal and linear refinements discouraged him from working in this medium.

With few and minor exceptions, all of Picasso's prints from 1897 to 1945—nearly fifty years of graphics activity—were confined to black and white, despite the artist's parallel development over this period as a brilliant colorist in painting and sculpture. In this sense, Picasso was holding fast to the classic roots of printmaking and the tradition of his fellow countryman, Francisco Goya—a graphic tradition of pure and "biting" black on white, unadorned by the distraction of color.

Figure 2.
Picasso:
Young Woman Facing Left, Three-Quarter View.
Woodcut. 1906.

Lithography, a "planographic" or flat technique, utilizes polished slabs of limestone or its substitute, zinc plates, on which the image is drawn with oil-base crayon or ink. The surrounding areas are moistened and printers ink is rolled onto the surface. The ink adheres to the drawing, but not to the wet areas—the simple principle of oil not mixing with water. As a result, the printed image is almost identical to the drawn version. Picasso had executed about twenty lithographs from 1919 until the Liberation in 1945, but none in color. The most productive period of his work in lithography began with his experiments in 1945, in the old printmaking atelier of Fernand Mourlot. Here, Picasso, often to the amazement of Mourlot and his master printers, defied old rules and administered to the stone or zinc in a manner never seen before. Guided by Mourlot's expertise, and taking full advantage of the spontaneity that lithography permits, Picasso created many multi-color prints. One of his most ambitious attempts, in six colors, is *Figure with Striped Blouse* of 1949 (fig. 3). But this print, like many of his more complicated color lithographs, was executed on "transfer" paper, then transposed to the stone or plate—a method of convenience that somewhat separates the artist from the graphic process.

Figure 3.
Picasso:
Figure with Striped Blouse.
Lithograph. 1949.

The Move South and the Linocut. In 1958, Picasso purchased the Château de Vauvenargues, on the northern slopes of Mont Sainte-Victoire near Aix-en-Provence. Soon afterwards, he married Jacqueline Roque. At that time, he was also working in his villa, "La Californie," at Cannes and for several years he and Jacqueline lived alternately in these two southern environments, far from the bustle of Paris. They were also far from the Parisian print ateliers, where, when Picasso was *en ville,* proofs of the varying "states" in the development of his prints (sometimes as many as thirty for the lithographs) were made overnight for his corrections and approvals. Now, in the south, Picasso found himself impatient with the delays and precious time lost between execution on the plate or stone and the final return of proofs from Paris. Creative continuity was broken; the artist, we can theorize, was hoping for a new circumstance that would permit him speed and more direct control over the many sequences in the development of a color print.

As early as 1951, Picasso had made annual linocut posters for the Expositions and bullfights at Vallauris, assisted by a Vallauris printer, Arnéra. The majority of these posters, similar to Matisse's early linocut (fig. 1) and Picasso's own first linocut, *The Squab* (fig. 4), of 1939, consisted simply of negative light lines against a dark background. Several, however, employed colors abundantly and their gaiety and forcefulness must have pleased Picasso. Also at Vallauris, in 1947, the artist had begun to work with ceramics, with Suzanne and Georges Ramié, discovering new technical and artistic possibilities in this ancient art and enjoying the intimate relationship of artist and craftsman-collaborator within the small village workshop. Eleven years later, in 1958, Picasso again sought out the master printer Arnéra in nearby Vallauris, and began what was to become an epic initial series of forty-five multi-colored linocuts and a total production of over one hundred linocuts by 1963.

Figure 4.
Picasso: *The Squab.* Linocut. 1939.

The first linocut of this series and by far the most ambitious one to that date, marking the first attempt by Picasso to use linocut for complex imagery, was *Bust of a Woman, after Cranach the Younger.* (Plate 14).

Picasso was already familiar with the basic advantage of a linoleum cutting: the ease of producing in the soft material a continuous, almost fluid stroke that can make curvilinear bands and patterns. Furthermore, linocut printing, even more than lithography, where over-inking can cause design disfigurement, leaves a rather thick layer of ink on the paper, more akin to the silkscreen technique. Picasso now observed in his Cranach print that when several colors are printed, one on top of another, a tactile, "painterly" quality results. In addition, the edges of each color area and the oily surface of the ink itself visually change in different lights, as in oil paintings with impasto. These effects, and the luminosity of the colors themselves, juxtaposed and overlaid, must have excited him greatly, holding a multiple-image potential of a painterly nature never before attained. But despite its success and the encouragement it gave, the Cranach print revealed certain limitations inherent in the multi-color process that conflicted with the very virtues of the linocut.

Picasso had wanted six colors with which he could improvise on the theme of the sixteenth-century portrait. To obtain them, he did what graphic artists have been doing since the early sixteenth century—he cut a separate block for each color. The Renaissance artists and cutters had gone through this somewhat redundant procedure to make their chiaroscuro color prints, the Rococo engravers had suffered a similar discipline for their elaborate color aquatints, and the French painter-lithographers of the late-nineteenth century and the German expressionist woodcutters of this century had done the same. But with his six-color linocut print, Picasso had experienced a discontinuity in having to cut each color area on a different block. This separateness of action slowed down the creative act—which had been accelerated by the nature of the soft material—and tended to dismember it. For many of Picasso's color lithographs, Mourlot, in Paris, had previously made the color "separations" direct from the transfer paper on which the artist worked. In the case of the linocut, however, the necessity of designing and cutting each block for correct registration (seeing that all the color elements, whether thin lines or large areas, were expertly superimposed in successive printings) was unavoidable by the artist and taxing both on artist and printer. All these problems are evidenced in the Cranach print. Out of what likely had been a frustrating experience, and wanting to continue to refine and expand his work in linoleum, which now gave full indication of its color and design potential, Picasso invented, by sheer creative necessity, a new method of multi-color graphics—all colors printed from one and the same block.[1]

From One Block, Many Colors. To fully understand the new process which Picasso adopted for all of his linocuts after the Cranach portrait (over one hundred prints) let us analyze a specific linocut: the *Picador and Bull* of 1959, the third print made by the artist using the one-block principle.[2] For proper visualization of the step-by-step development, the print has been "separated" into its four colors and the successive states are shown in the sequence in which they were cut, inked and printed. Therefore, the illustrations serve as a "motion study" of Picasso's linocut technique. In the following discussion, the reader should refer periodically to Plate 5, the illustration of the completed work.

It can reasonably be assumed that Picasso began with a colored drawing of the composition, probably in gouache, which served as a model for drawing on the block and for the cutting and inking. The uncut block, with the first color, ochre, rolled on the entire face of the linoleum, is seen in fig. 6. A proof impression is printed, or "pulled," of this first state to make certain that the color is correct. Then the complete edition (usually fifty impressions plus a few proofs for the artist) is pulled from the block. In nearly all of Picasso's linocuts, this first printing covers the whole picture area with color. The rare exception is when the artist masks out areas, usually well into the center of the composition, with cutout patterns of paper placed on the block. After inking, the paper is removed and the block placed in the press. The areas that were masked and therefore uninked thus appear white, the color of the paper, but can still be overprinted later since these same areas of the block itself have not yet been cut away. The first printing of the overall basic color points up another difference between color lithography and color linocuts as executed by Picasso. In the lithographs, quite often much of the white paper remains unprinted, usually as a background. The elements of color are worked into what might be termed a "white atmosphere." In the Picasso linocuts, colors nearly always dwell within a total color environment; the new linocut process dictates the aesthetic basis of the print itself—color from edge to edge.

In the next step the artist presumably brushed onto the block, still inked with ochre, the second color, using his drawing as a guide. Then he cut away *all* of the areas on the block still showing the ochre. This done, the light brown printer's ink was rolled over the remaining raised portions of the block, resulting in what can be seen in fig. 7. Notice the fine engraved lines that form an outer contour, a second silhouette of the bull, within the first. These lines are key to the second and third cuttings; they serve as guides and also enable the ochre to come through, outlining the subsequently printed black inner design. This key engraved line is analogous to similar lines on Greek vase paintings. The ancient artists incised through the black colored slip to reach the basic terra cotta of the vase (fig. 5). Indeed, Picasso may have been influenced by such practices, common to ancient Mediterranean cultures. In many of his linocuts, even the colors are similar to those

Figure 5.
Greek Vase Painting
(Black Figure)

in the vase paintings—*Picador and Bull* being typical. Such colors, for Picasso, were as basic as the earth itself; these rich terra cottas and siennas dominate the landscape at Vauvenargues and are also in the oldest of color prints—the early sixteenth-century Italian chiaroscuro woodcuts.

The second state proof is now pulled from this first cutting; when satisfactory to the artist, the edition is again put through the press and the light brown pattern is imprinted over the ochre background (fig. 8).

The artist now brushes the dark brown patterns onto the block, over the light brown inked areas still retained on the uncut portion of the block. He then cuts away all of the surface containing the light brown ink, leaving only the dark brown (fig. 9). A third state proof is pulled, after dark brown ink has been rolled on. This proof shows the dark brown printed over the light brown and ochre. When this proof has been approved, the edition is put through the press for the third time (fig. 10).

A similar sequence is followed with the last color, black (fig. 11), and the edition is printed for the fourth and last time (fig. 12). The print, in fact the whole edition, is completed!

There is a very important distinction between the many work proofs already described as integral to Picasso's development of the linocut, and what is normally a proof when using a separate block or plate for each color (the sole practice before Picasso's invention). Conventionally, an artist not only has the advantage of proofing each block or color state, as Picasso must have done with his linocuts, but more important, of proofing *all of the colors printed together,* since each block or plate is retained. Quite often, after scrutiny of this full-color proof, there are corrections on one or more of the blocks. The artist is finally given a proof that he considers acceptable; this one becomes what is traditionally known as the "bon à tirer," and the edition is pulled to match in all respects this approved example. With the one-block practice, such proofing is impossible, since the entire edition must be pulled for each color, separately, before cutting away a given area for the next color.

With the one-block method, the artist can view and correct the work only as it develops *progressively*. He cannot backtrack. This irrevocability of the creative process and its results are unique in the graphic arts, and perhaps without analogy in other art forms. It is a strange and almost mystical recipe, reflecting the extraordinary wherewithal and confidence of the aging master. The one hundred linocuts illustrated in this book were all printed in editions of fifty. Thus, in a period of five years, from 1958 through 1963, Picasso "brought into the world" five thousand large-scale, brilliantly executed, painting-like, original graphic works. What a marvelous gift to the world, this vast progeny at the age of eighty-two!

Bullfights and Bacchanals. Some of the artist's most personal subject matter and symbols abound in these linocuts. Like so much of Picasso's art, there is a cyclical and serial aspect to them. He repeatedly explores the bullfight, for example: this confrontation being part of his deep cultural past, rekindled by its introduction at Vallauris in 1954, where, significant to Picasso's humanism, killing the bull is prohibited. Picasso expresses the subject with a thoroughness that recalls the aquatints and lithographs of his countryman, Francisco Goya, but without the bitter violence. No other series of graphic works, aside from Goya's, explores with such range the duality of man and beast in the arena.

The musical aspect of Picasso's art prevails in many of the linocuts. In his Bacchanal subjects, satyrs play their flutes, but far more suggestive of sound are the designs themselves, buoyant and patterned to psychologically bridge the gap between eye and ear. The blithesomeness of these scenes does not extinguish the classic dignity achieved by the balance of composition and the elegant drawing. The expansive imagination of the artist roams from the wide-angle openness of pastoral scenes down the scale to haunting close-ups of still life, instantly activated by hovering light bulbs. It is the idea materialized, the life-giving force symbolized (we are reminded of the great electric light in the mural *Guernica*). Artists and models strategically confront each other; so do the surreal "picnickers" after Manet's painting. Portraits defy time and space, coiffures and costumes are interchangeable, angles of view are vicarious. Old master paintings are improvised upon and clowns facially articulate their comedy. When viewing these many linocuts, with their calligraphic and narrative intensities, we realize how diverse is the artist's expressionism. The extraordinary accomplishment, eclipsing the importance of the one-block invention itself, is the achievement of a unified style. The pervading "decorative" motif, heightened by color, rather than softening the expressionistic edge, proceeds to embody and amplify it. This complete fusion of expressionist and design forces is the creative mix that is Picasso's signal contribution.

DONALD H. KARSHAN

FOOTNOTES

1. Attempts have been made, though rarely successful, to apply different colors onto the same plate or block for a single printing. Derain brushed different colors onto each of his woodblocks. 'A la poupée," in which color is applied by dabbing the surface of the plate with an inked cloth, was used with exquisite results by Mary Cassatt, in combination with her aquatint and drypoint work. But the application had to be repeated for each impression, resulting in variations from print to print. The monotype process is the actual painting on a metal or glass plate, which is then imprinted on paper. Degas and Prendergast used this technique with great success. But in both cases, the color is not being printed from a fixed condition that can be repeated mechanically.

2. There is no indication that other artists have worked with the one-block multi-color technique since Picasso introduced it a decade ago. Perhaps this clarification of the technique will encourage its further utilization as a graphic medium.

6.

7.

8.

9.

10.

11.

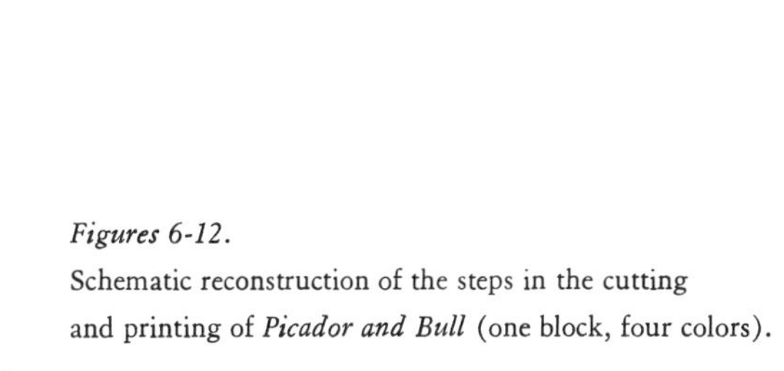

Figures 6-12.
Schematic reconstruction of the steps in the cutting and printing of *Picador and Bull* (one block, four colors).

12.

SELECTED BIBLIOGRAPHY

1. Adhémar, Jean, *La Gravure Originale du XX*[e] Siecle. Paris, Edition Aimery Somogy, 1967.

2. Adrian, Dennis, "Picasso the Printmaker," *Picasso in Chicago,* Art Institute of Chicago, 1968.

3. Berggruen & Cie., *Picasso, 60 Ans de Gravures.* Paris, 1964.

4. Bloch, Georges, *Picasso, Catalogue of the Printed Graphic Work 1904-1967.* (Trilingual edition with 1592 illustrations and a bibliography of 134 books illustrated by Picasso. Based on the comprehensive Picasso exhibition at the Kunsthaus, Zurich.) Published in Bern, Kornfeld and Klipstein, 1958. Distributed by Office du Livre, Fribourg, Switzerland.

5. Boeck, Wilhelm, *Picasso Linoleum Cuts: Bacchanals, Women, Bulls & Bullfighters.* New York, Harry N. Abrams, Inc., 1962.

6. Brunner, Felix, *A Handbook of Graphic Reproduction Processes.* Teufen, Switzerland, Arthur Niggli, 1962 (1st ed.), 1964 (2nd ed.).

7. Geiser, Berhard, *Picasso, Fifty-five Years of His Graphic Work.* (Biography and Documentation by Hans Bollinger.) New York, Harry N. Abrams, Inc., 1965.

8. Geiser, Berhard, *Picasso, 45 Gravures sur Linoleum, 1958-1960.* Paris, Galerie Louise Leiris, 1960.

9. Leonhard, Kurt, *Pablo Picasso: Recent Etchings, Lithographs, and Linoleum Cuts.* Biography and Documentation by Hans Bollinger. Translated by Norbert Guterman. New York, Harry N. Abrams, Inc., 1967.

10. Los Angeles County Museum of Art, *Picasso: Sixty Years of Graphic Works.* Los Angeles, 1966.

Abbreviation used in this work:
[B] = Berggruen (Bibliography No. 3). Berggruen catalogue numbers and French titles are included in the plate identifications.

Picasso Linocuts 1958-1963

HEAD OF A WOMAN
(Tête de femme)
1962.
1 block.
25¼ x 21 inches. (B. 326)

THE LUNCHEON ON THE GRASS *(Le déjeuner sur l'herbe)*, 1962.
1 block. 21 x 25¼ inches. (B. 366)

HEAD OF A WOMAN IN PROFILE
(Tête de femme de profil)
1959.
1 block: black, mauve and beige.
25¼ x 21 inches. (B. 274)

PICADOR AND BULLFIGHTER *(Picador et torero)*, 1959.
1 block: black, mauve and beige. 21 x 25¼ inches. (B. 275)

PICADOR AND BULL *(Picador et taureau)*, 1959.
1 block: black, mauve, brown and beige. 21 x 25¼ inches. (B. 276)

BULLFIGHT *(Pique)*, 1959.
1 block: red and yellow. 21 x 25¼ inches. (B. 277)

BULLFIGHT *(Pique)*, 1959.
1 block: black, mauve and beige. 21 x 25¼ inches. (B. 278)

AFTER THE LANCE *(Après la pique)*, 1959.
1 block: black, mauve and beige. 21 x 25¼ inches. (B. 279)

BULLFIGHT *(Pique)*, 1959.
1 block: black, mauve, brown and beige. 21 x 25¼ inches. (B. 280)

PICADOR AND HORSE
(Picador et cheval)
1959.
1 block: black and brown.
25¼ x 21 inches. (B. 281)

STILL LIFE UNDER THE LAMP *(Nature morte sous la lampe)*, 1962.
1 block. 21 x 25¼ inches. (B. 357)

BUST OF A WOMAN, AFTER CRANACH THE YOUNGER
(Buste de femme, d'après Cranach le Jeune)
1958.
6 blocks.
25½ x 21 inches. (B. 273)

BEARDED MAN WITH CROWN OF LEAVES
(Homme barbu couronné de feuillage)
1962.
1 block.
13¾ x 10¾ inches. (B. 346)

BUST OF A WOMAN WITH A HAT
(Buste de femme au chapeau)
1962.
1 block.
25¼ x 21 inches. (B. 325)

PICADOR, WOMAN AND HORSE
(Picador, femme et cheval)
1959.
1 block: black and grege.
25¼ x 21 inches. (B. 282)

THE VASE OF FLOWERS
(Le vase de fleurs)
1959.
1 block: black, mauve, brown and beige.
25¼ x 21 inches. (B. 283)

RECLINING WOMAN AND MAN WITH A GUITAR *(Femme couchée et homme à la guitare)*, 1959.
1 block: black, mauve and beige. 21 x 25¼ inches. (B. 285)

WOMAN IN AN ARMCHAIR AND GUITARIST *(Femme dans un fauteuil et guitariste)*, 1959.
1 block: black, brown and beige. 21 x 25¼ inches. (B. 286)

RECLINING WOMAN AND GUITARIST *(Femme couchée et guitariste)*, 1959.
1 block: black, brown and beige. 21 x 25¼ inches. (B. 287)

RECLINING WOMAN AND MAN WITH A LARGE HAT *(Femme couchée et homme au grand chapeau)*, 1959.
1 block: black, brown and beige. 21 x 25¼ inches. (B. 288)

TWO WOMEN NEAR A WINDOW *(Deux femmes près de la fenêtre)*, 1959.
1 block: black, brown and beige. 21 x 25¼ inches. (B. 293)

WOMAN LOOKING OUT THE WINDOW *(Femme regardant par la fenêtre)*, 1959.
1 block: black, brown and beige. 21 x 25¼ inches. (B. 294)

DANAE *(Danaé)*, 1962.
1 block. 10¾ x 13¾ inches. (B. 348)

WOMAN WITH HAT
(Femme au chapeau)
1962.
1 block.
13¾ x 10¾ inches. (B. 329)

THREE WOMEN *(Trois femmes)*, 1959.
1 block: black, brown and beige. 21 x 25¼ inches. (B. 295)

BACCHANAL *(Bacchanale)*, 1959.
1 block: black and grege. 21 x 25¼ inches. (B. 296)

WOMAN WITH A NECKLACE
(Femme au collier)
1959.
1 block: black, brown and beige.
25¼ x 21 inches. (B. 297)

MOTHER, DANCER AND MUSICIAN
(Mère, danseur et musicien)
1959.
1 block: black, brown and beige.
25¼ x 21 inches. (B. 298)

BACCHANAL *(Bacchanale)*, 1959.
1 block: black, brown, blue and beige. 21 x 25¼ inches. (B. 299)

BACCHANAL WITH BULL *(Bacchanale au taureau)*, 1959.
1 block: black, green, blue and beige. 21 x 25¼ inches. (B. 302)

DANCERS WITH OWL *(Les danseurs au hibou)*, 1959.
1 block: black and brown. 21 x 25¼ inches. (B. 305)

THE GRAPE GATHERERS *(Les vendangeurs)*, 1959.
1 block: black, mauve, brown and beige. 21 x 25¼ inches. (B. 306)

THE BROKEN LANCE *(La pique cassée)*, 1959.
1 block. 21 x 25¼ inches. (B. 290)

BACCHANAL *(Bacchanale)*, 1959.
1 block. 21 x 25¼ inches. (B. 300)

HEAD OF A WOMAN, BROWN
(Tête de femme, brun)
1962.
1 block.
25¼ x 21 inches. (B. 327)

TWO WOMEN *(Deux femmes)*, 1959.
1 block. 21 x 25¼ inches. (B. 284)

BACCHANAL WITH OWL *(Bacchanale au hibou)*, 1959.
1 block: black and grege. 21 x 25¼ inches. (B. 307)

DANCERS AND MUSICIAN *(Danseurs et musicien)*, 1959.
1 block: black and grege. 21 x 25¼ inches. (B. 308)

THE BANDERILLAS *(Les banderilles)*, 1959.
1 block: black, brown and beige. 21 x 25¼ inches. (B. 309)

BEFORE THE LANCE *(Avant la pique)*, 1959.
1 block: black, brown and beige. 21 x 25¼ inches. (B. 310)

PICADOR, 1959.
1 block: black, brown and beige. 6½ x 9 inches. (B. 311)

BANDERILLAS *(Banderilles)*, 1959.
1 block: black, brown and beige. 6½ x 9 inches. (B. 312)

LANCE *(Pique)*, 1959.
1 block: black, brown and beige. 6½ x 9 inches. (B. 313)

FAROL, 1959.
1 block: black, brown and beige. $6\frac{1}{2}$ x 9 inches. (B. 314)

WOMAN LEANING ON ELBOWS
(Femme accoudée)
1959.
1 block.
25¼ x 21 inches. (B. 291)

FAUNS AND GOAT *(Faunes et chèvre)*, 1959.
1 block. 21 x 25¼ inches. (B. 303)

BEFORE THE LANCE *(Avant la pique)*, 1959.
1 block: black, brown and beige. 6½ x 9 inches. (B. 315)

HEAD OF A WOMAN
(Tête de femme)
1959-1960.
1 block: black, brown and beige.
26 x 21¼ inches. (B. 316)

PLANT WITH LITTLE BULLS
(Plante aux toritos)
1959-1960.
1 block: blue, brown and beige.
26 x 21¼ inches. (B. 317)

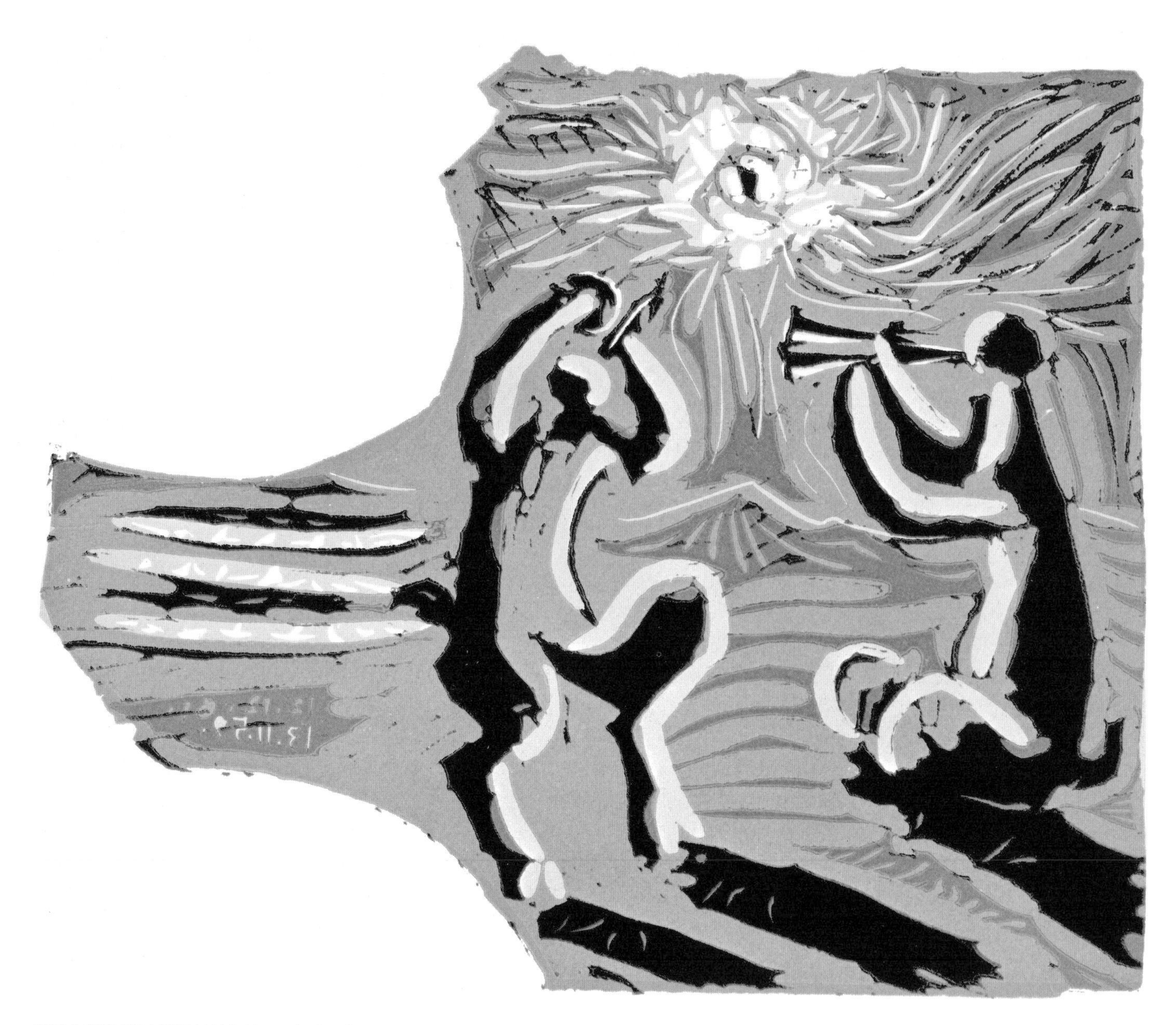

THE LITTLE BACCHANAL *(La petite bacchanale)*, 1959-1961.
1 block: black, brown and beige, 8¾ x 10¼ inches. (B. 319)

LUNCH ON THE GRASS *(Le déjeuner sur l'herbe)*, 1961.
1 block: black only. 21 x 25¼ inches. (B. 320)

HEAD OF A FAUN
(Tête de faune)
1962.
1 block: black and brown.
25¼ x 21 inches. (B. 324)

HEAD OF A BOY
(Tête de garçon)
1962.
1 block: black only.
13¾ x 10¾ inches. (B. 330)

HEAD OF A BOY
(Tête de garçon)
1962.
1 block: black only.
13¾ x 10¾ inches. (B. 331)

BUST OF A WOMAN
(Buste de femme)
1962.
1 block: black only.
13¾ x 10¾ inches. (B. 332)

LARGE HEAD OF WOMAN WITH HAT
(Grande tête de femme au chapeau)
1962.
1 block: black, dark brown, light brown and beige.
25¼ x 21 inches. (B. 334)

LUNCH ON THE GRASS *(Le déjeuner sur l'herbe)*, 1962.
1 block: black, brown and beige. 21 x 25¼ inches. (B. 336)

WOMAN WITH FLOWING HAIR
(Femme aux cheveux flous)
1962.
1 block: black, brown and beige.
13¾ x 10¾ inches. (B. 337)

THE GLASS UNDER THE LAMP
(Le verre sous la lampe)
1962.
1 block: black, gray and beige.
13¾ x 10¾ inches. (B. 338)

WOMAN WITH HAT
(Femme au chapeau)
1962.
1 block: black, dark brown, light brown and beige.
13¾ x 10¾ inches. (B. 339)

BEARDED MAN WITH CROWN
(Homme barbu couronné)
1962.
1 block: black, brown and beige.
13¾ x 10¾ inches. (B. 340)

WOMAN WITH HAIR BAND
(Femme au bandeau)
1962.
1 block: black, dark brown, light brown and beige.
13¾ x 10¾ inches. (B. 341)

BACCHANAL WITH BLACK BULL *(Bacchanale au taureau noir)*, 1959.
1 block. 21 x 25¼ inches. (B. 304)

LANCE *(Pique)*, 1959.
1 block. 21 x 25¼ inches. (B. 289)

FACE
(Visage)
1962.
1 block: black and brown.
13¾ x 10¾ inches. (B. 342)

YOUNG MAN WITH CROWN
(Jeune homme couronné)
1962.
1 block: black, light brown, dark brown and beige.
13¾ x 10¾ inches. (B. 343)

WOMAN WITH A FLOWERED HAT
(Femme au chapeau à fleurs)
1962.
1 block: black and beige.
13¾ x 10¾ inches. (B. 344)

SEATED WOMAN WITH CHIGNON
(Femme assise au chignon)
1962.
1 block: black, brown, light beige and dark beige.
13¾ x 10¾ inches. (B. 345)

SLEEPING WOMAN *(Femme endormie)*, 1962.
1 block: black, brown and beige. 10¾ x 13¾ inches. (B. 347)

HEAD OF A WOMAN
(Tête de femme)
1962.
1 block: black, brown and beige.
25¼ x 21 inches. (B. 349)

LARGE HEAD OF A WOMAN WITH DECORATED HAT
(Grande tête de femme au chapeau orné)
1962.
1 block: black and beige.
25¼ x 21 inches. (B. 350)

LARGE RED, BLUE AND YELLOW HEAD
(Grande tête rouge, bleu, jaune)
1962.
1 block: black, red, blue, yellow and beige.
25¼ x 21 inches. (B. 351)

BACCHANAL *(Bacchanale)*, 1959.
1 block. 21 x 25¼ inches. (B. 301)

WOMAN WITH HAT
(Femme au chapeau)
1962.
1 block.
13¾ x 10¾ inches. (B. 333)

HEAD OF A WOMAN
(Tête de femme)
1962.
1 block.
25¼ x 21 inches. (B. 335)

JACQUELINE
1959.
1 block.
25¼ x 21 inches. (B. 292)

STILL LIFE WITH A BOTTLE
(Nature morte à la bouteille)
1962.
1 block: black only.
25¼ x 21 inches. (B. 352)

STILL LIFE WITH A BOTTLE
(Nature morte à la bouteille)
1962.
1 block: black, brown and gray.
25¼ x 21 inches. (B. 353)

LARGE HEAD OF A WOMAN
(Grande tête de femme)
1962.
1 block: black, dark brown, light brown and beige.
25¼ x 21 inches. (B. 354)

NUDE WOMAN AT THE SPRING *(Femme nue à la source)*, 1962.
1 block: black, dark brown, light brown and beige. 21 x 25¼ inches. (B. 356)

SMALL BUST OF A WOMAN
(Petit buste de femme)
1962.
1 block: black, brown and beige.
13¾ x 10¾ inches. (B. 358)

LUNCH ON THE GRASS
(Le déjeuner sur l'herbe)
1962.
1 block: black, brown and beige.
13¾ x 10¾ inches. (B. 359)

WOMAN WITH FLOWERED HAT
(Femme au chapeau à fleurs)
1962.
1 block: black, brown and beige.
13¾ x 10¾ inches. (B. 360)

NUDE WOMAN PICKING FLOWERS
(Femme nue cueillant des fleurs)
1962.
1 block: black, brown and beige.
13¾ x 10¾ inches. (B. 361)

SPANISH WOMAN
(L'Espagnole)
1962.
1 block: black, brown and beige.
13¾ x 10¾ inches. (B. 362)

WOMAN WITH FLOWING HAIR
(Femme aux cheveux flous)
1962.
1 block: black and beige.
13¾ x 10¾ inches. (B. 363)

SEATED NUDE WOMAN
(Femme nue assise)
1962.
1 block: black, brown and beige.
13¾ x 10¾ inches. (B. 364)

SMALL HEAD OF A WOMAN, CROWNED
(Petite tête de femme, couronnée)
1962.
1 block: black, dark brown, light brown and beige.
13¾ x 10¾ inches. (B. 365)

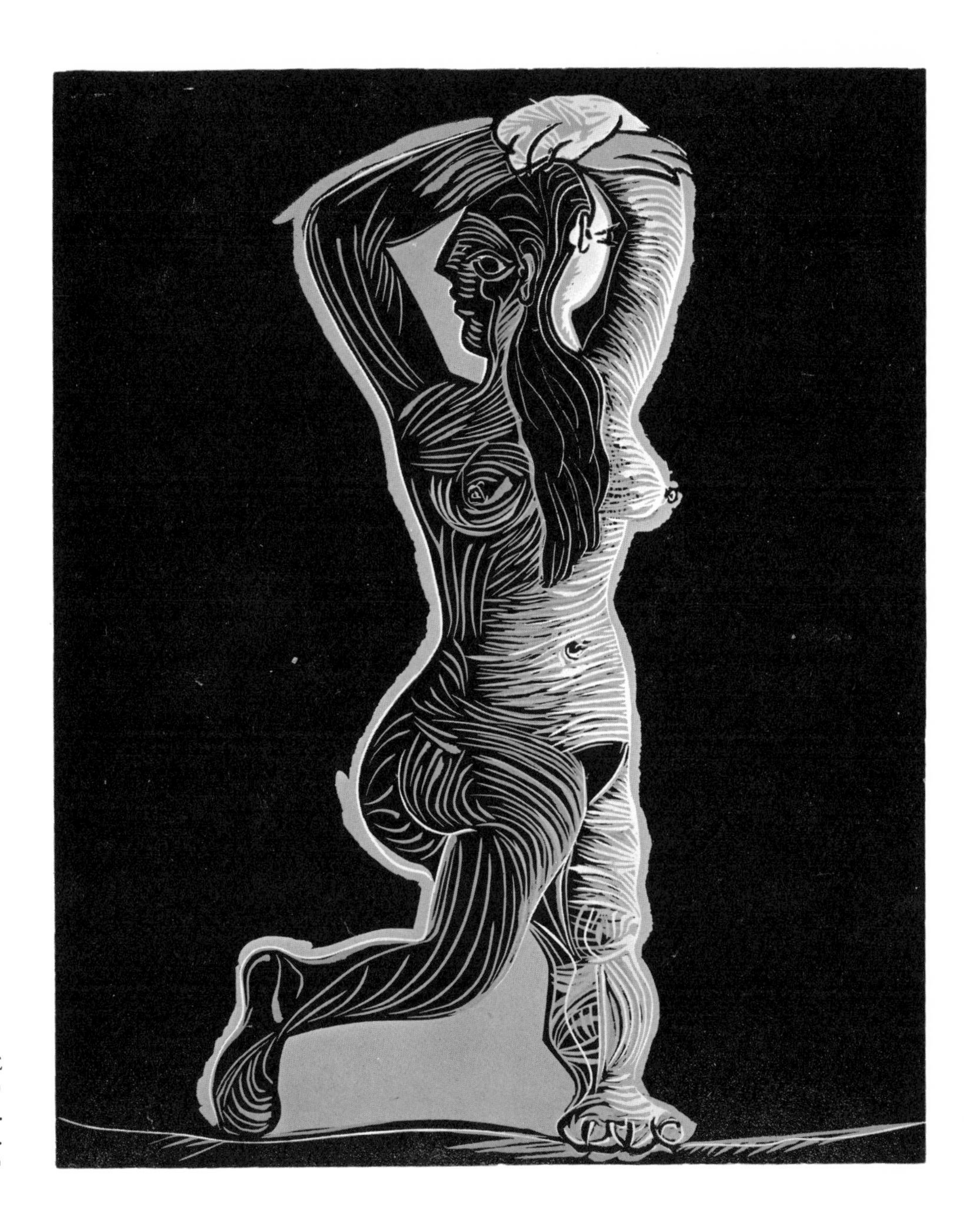

LARGE FEMALE NUDE
(Grand nu de femme)
1962.
1 block: black, brown and beige.
25¼ x 21 inches. (B. 367)

MAN WITH A RUFF COLLAR
(L'Homme à la fraise)
1963.
1 block: black, brown, blue-gray and gray.
21 x 15¾ inches. (B. 368)

LADY WITH A RUFF COLLAR
(La dame à la collerette)
1963.
1 block: black, brown, blue-gray and gray.
21 x 15¾ inches. (B. 369)

FAMILY SCENE *(Scène familiale)*, 1963.
1 block: black and brown. 15¾ x 21 inches. (B. 370)

WOMAN WITH A HAT
(La femme au chapeau)
1963.
1 block.
21 x 15¾ inches. (B. 376)

STILL LIFE UNDER THE LAMP
(Nature morte sous la lampe)
1962.
1 block.
25¼ x 21 inches. (B. 355)

HEAD OF A WOMAN
(Tête de femme)
1962.
1 block.
25¼ x 21 inches. (B. 328)

THE FLOWERED HAT
(Le chapeau à fleurs)
1963.
1 block.
21 x 15¾ inches. (B. 371)

HEADS
(Têtes)
1963.
1 block: black, brown and beige.
25¼ x 21 inches. (B. 372)

MAN WITH A STICK
(L'Homme au baton)
1963.
1 block: black, brown and beige.
25¼ x 21 inches. (B. 373)

STANDING NUDE WOMAN
(Femme nue debout)
1963.
1 block: black, brown and beige.
25¼ x 21 inches. (B. 374)

HEAD
(Tête)
1963.
1 block: black and beige.
25¼ x 21 inches. (B. 375)

LIST OF PLATES

In color: Plates 1, 2, 11, 12, 13, 14, 23, 24, 33, 34, 35, 36, 45, 46, 63, 64, 73, 74, 75, 76, 93, 94, 95, 96

51. LUNCH ON THE GRASS, 1961.
52. HEAD OF A FAUN, 1962.
53. HEAD OF A BOY, 1962.
54. HEAD OF A BOY, 1962.
55. BUST OF A WOMAN, 1962.
56. LARGE HEAD OF WOMAN WITH HAT, 1962.
57. LUNCH ON THE GRASS, 1962.
58. WOMAN WITH FLOWING HAIR, 1962.
59. THE GLASS UNDER THE LAMP, 1962.
60. WOMAN WITH HAT, 1962.
61. BEARDED MAN WITH CROWN, 1962.
62. WOMAN WITH HAIR BAND, 1962.
63. BACCHANAL WITH BLACK BULL, 1959.
64. LANCE, 1959.
65. FACE, 1962.
66. YOUNG MAN WITH CROWN, 1962.
67. WOMAN WITH A FLOWERED HAT, 1962.
68. SEATED WOMAN WITH CHIGNON, 1962.
69. SLEEPING WOMAN, 1962.
70. HEAD OF A WOMAN, 1962.
71. LARGE HEAD OF A WOMAN WITH DECORATED HAT, 1962.
72. LARGE RED, BLUE AND YELLOW HEAD, 1962.
73. BACCHANAL, 1959.
74. WOMAN WITH HAT, 1962.
75. HEAD OF A WOMAN, 1962.
76. JACQUELINE, 1959.
77. STILL LIFE WITH A BOTTLE, 1962.
78. STILL LIFE WITH A BOTTLE, 1962.
79. LARGE HEAD OF A WOMAN, 1962.
80. NUDE WOMAN AT THE SPRING, 1962.
81. SMALL BUST OF A WOMAN, 1962.
82. LUNCH ON THE GRASS, 1962.
83. WOMAN WITH FLOWERED HAT, 1962.
84. NUDE WOMAN PICKING FLOWERS, 1962.
85. SPANISH WOMAN, 1962.
86. WOMAN WITH FLOWING HAIR, 1962.
87. SEATED NUDE WOMAN, 1962.
88. SMALL HEAD OF A WOMAN, CROWNED, 1962.
89. LARGE FEMALE NUDE, 1962.
90. MAN WITH A RUFF COLLAR, 1963.
91. LADY WITH A RUFF COLLAR, 1963.
92. FAMILY SCENE, 1963.
93. WOMAN WITH A HAT, 1963.
94. STILL LIFE UNDER THE LAMP, 1962.
95. HEAD OF A WOMAN, 1962.
96. THE FLOWERED HAT, 1963.
97. HEADS, 1963.
98. MAN WITH A STICK, 1963.
99. STANDING NUDE WOMAN, 1963.
100. HEAD, 1963.

Book design by Alfred Campisi
Text type: 11 point Granjon
Display type: Palatino
Color plates from the original linocuts were made and printed by Triton Press, New York, July, 1968
Black and white reproductions were printed by New Era Lithograph Company, Plainview, N.Y.